ALSO BY WILSON THE PUG WITH NANCY LEVINE

The Tao of Pug
Homer for the Holidays
Letters to a Young Pug

The Ugly Pugling

WILSON THE PUG IN LOVE

WILSON THE PUG WITH NANCY LEVINE

Skyhorse Publishing

First published in 2007 by Viking Studio, a member of Penguin Group (USA) Inc.

Skyhorse Publishing books may be purchased in bulk at special discounts for sales promotion, corporate gifts, fund-raising, or educational purposes. Special editions can also be created to specifications. For details, contact the Special Sales Department, Skyhorse Publishing, 307 West 36th Street, 11th Floor, New York, NY 10018 or info@skyhorsepublishing.com.

Skyhorse® and Skyhorse Publishing® are registered trademarks of Skyhorse Publishing, Inc.®, a Delaware corporation.

Visit our website at www.skyhorsepublishing.com.

10 9 8 7 6 5 4 3 2 1

Library of Congress Cataloging-in-Publication Data is available on file.

Cover design by Daniel Lagin
Cover photograph by Nancy Levine

Print ISBN: 978-1-5107-1444-1
Ebook ISBN: 978-1-5107-1448-9

Printed in China

For you, O my Best Beloved

Introduction

Hello. My name is Wilson the Pug. As some of you may know, I am a Taoist pug, descended from a long lineage of Taoist pugs, dating back to around 500 B.C. in ancient China. Way back then, my greatest great grandfather Pug-tzu was the canine companion and inspiration for Lao-tzu, the wise old philosopher who wrote the Tao-te Ching, the ancient Chinese book of wisdom.

It was during the writing of the classic text that Lao-tzu and Pug-tzu both found true love. It happened one day while Pug-tzu and Lao-tzu were lounging in a field of lilies not far from their village. Lao-tzu was pondering a philosophical dilemma and looked into Pug-tzu's deep brown eyes as he always did when trying to solve a puzzle.

"Oh my little puggled friend," said Lao-tzu, "my Tao-te Ching is all but complete except for a word on love. What shall we say?"

Just then a fair widow from the village happened to wander into the same field with her companion dog, a huge but gentle beast named Woo. The fair widow and her dog stopped and bade them a sweet hello. Lao-tzu was instantly smitten with the widow, as Pug-tzu was with the giant Woo. The lovely lady and her companion passed through the field and out of sight as if an apparition of beauty.

Lao-tzu and Pug-tzu stared at each other, open-mouthed, dumbfounded, as if struck by Cupid-tzu's arrow. Lao-tzu wondered aloud, "She is so beautiful. She would never be interested in a plain old man like me. What shall I do, little pug, as I feel myself instantly smitten, though impossibly so?"

Pug-tzu stared back into his friend's eyes and cocked his head from side to side as pugs are wont to do.

"Yes! You are right again, my wrinkled-browed friend!" as the old man scribbled a note onto a tiny piece of parchment for inclusion in his Tao-te Ching. *"The Master acts on what he feels and not what he sees."*

Lao-tzu and Pug-tzu returned to their village, where the old man conjured up the courage to call upon the fair widow. She told Lao-tzu she would welcome his company and wanted nothing more than to *"enjoy the plain and simple."* He included this thought in his book of wisdom as an homage to her.

Lao-tzu and Pug-tzu spent much time over the next several months appropriately courting the fair widow and her dog, Woo. In spite of their great differences in beauty and size, respectively, the couple's love prevailed, as it always does. Lao-tzu took the widow's hand in marriage and they spent the rest of their days together, Pug-tzu and Woo by their sides, a contented (though perhaps a mite quirky) family.

Inspired by his passion for Woo, Pug-tzu handed down this lesson of the ages to the pugs that followed. The wisdom of love was relayed from pug to pug to pug down through the years until it finally rested upon my furry shoulders.

This, then, is the story of how I met my true love, Hedy, and how I learned firsthand what happens when *the Master acts on what he feels and not what he sees*. Please, won't you join me?

—WILSON THE PUG

She was the most beautiful pug I'd ever seen.

I met Hedy one day in the park, quite by happenstance. We both stopped to sniff a certain savory spot in the grass, and when we looked up, our gazes locked as tightly as a crate door.

Hedy was unlike the other pugs I'd met before. With her big, floppy ears, prominent muzzle, and huge paws, she was a vision of loveliness.

We spent that day in the park, just lolling about in the grass.

Hedy whispered to me of her hopes and dreams. "Maybe someday we can share a plateful of cookies, " she said, revealing a deliciously robust appetite. Her soft snuffles played in my ear like a melody.

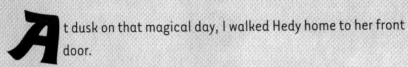t dusk on that magical day, I walked Hedy home to her front door.

"I had a wonderful time with you today," I told her. "May I see you again?"

"But Wilson," she said, "we are so very different. You are so handsome, and I am rather a homely pug."

"You are the fairest pug I have ever seen," I assured her. "Who is to say what is beautiful and what is not?"

And with this, we shared a kiss I shall never forget.

We met in the park again soon thereafter. I gave Hedy a yin-yang jacket that had belonged to my great grandmother pug. Legend had it that the jacket would fit only the pug who was destined to be my true love. It suited Hedy perfectly, as though it had been custom made for her.

She whispered, "Thank you, Wilson, the jacket is beautiful, and I will treasure it always," adding, "As it is written, *a kind heart makes the giving good.*"

knew then, without a doubt, I had found my true love.

But one day Hedy stopped coming to the park. Days became weeks. My curly tail wilted. I wondered what had happened to her.

I went to Hedy's house every day and sat in front of her door for hours. Little did I know that she was inside, staring out at me the whole time through the door's glass pane.

Something *had* happened to her.

Finally, I gave up and turned to walk away from her front door, my tail drooping behind me.

But as I was leaving, the door opened a crack. I stopped and looked back. Out stepped a huge dog, the biggest I'd ever seen. This, I assumed, was one of Hedy's housemates. Or perhaps a horse for the family carriage.

"Wait!" she called out to me.

Maybe she could tell me what had happened to Hedy, I thought as I turned back.

Noticing my look of perplexity—even more so than usual, as my wrinkles become accentuated when I'm confounded— she said, "Wilson, it's me, Hedy. See?" And she tried to squeeze into the yin-yang jacket I'd given her.

I gazed into her twinkling brown eyes and got a whiff of her sweetly biscuited breath. Sure enough, this was my Hedy after all. And my tail bounced back up like a daisy in the sun.

She told me of her life: "You see, Wilson, I'm not a homely pug at all. I'm a mastiff, and I have been bred for the show ring. Though I don't like show life at all, I can't help but win all the competitions because they judge mainly by appearance."

"My poor, beautiful Hedy," I said.

"Wait," she said, "it gets worse."

"**A**s soon as I win the Big Show, I will be crowned a champion and wedded to another mastiff, a brindle stud named Shakespeare." Hedy continued, "I don't care for Shakespeare a bit—he's rather uncouth. But it has all been arranged by the humans, so nothing can be done to change things."

I could not bear the thought of my Hedy being wed to this Shakespeare fellow. So I resolved to stop thinking for the time being.

We lounged on the lawn, and Hedy said, "Oh, Wilson, I love you and just want to *enjoy the plain and simple*."

"Hedy, my love for you is as great as I am small. *The Master acts on what he feels and not what he sees*. We will surely find a way to be together," though I didn't know how.

The next day, Hedy confided in her twin sister, Greta.

"Oh, Greta, what can I do? I have fallen head over heels for Wilson the Pug, but ours is an impossible love. Once I win the Big Show and am crowned a champion, I will be married off to Shakespeare forever."

Greta sighed, then said, "If only I were you, Hedy. You know how I have loved and pined for Shakespeare ever since we were pups. And oh, how I long to prance around the show ring as you do." She shook her head slowly, adding, "But I don't meet the mastiff standard for beauty as I am without 'marked wrinkles, which are particularly distinctive.' So I suppose neither the show ring nor Shakespeare will ever be mine."

Hedy assured her, "You are beautiful to me, Greta."

Meanwhile, I stopped by the pub where I figured I could find my best friend, Homer, who was a regular. It was the sort of place where everybody knows your name (as long as you're older than twenty-one in dog years).

"Homer," I told him, "I have fallen madly in love with Hedy the Mastiff. What's a pug to do?"

"Whoa, that's heavy," said Homer. "You just need to meet another pug to get your mind off her. C'mon, let's go to a pug party. I think Nelly the Pug will be there. She is so fine."

Homer and I went to a nearby pug party, where we were playing a little game of pug puppy in the middle. But I suddenly felt someone else's eyes upon us.

"Excuse me, boys," she said.

Homer looked up and said, "Oh hey, Nelly, you're looking mighty fine today. Grrr."

"Hi, Homer," said Nelly. "Actually, I wanted to talk to your friend Wilson. Alone, please, if you'll excuse us."

Nelly beckoned me over to her couch, which she liked to bring to parties.

She said, "Wilson, I've been seeing you at these parties for years and have read all your books. I must confess, I have a real crush on you."

"Nelly, I am so very flattered," I said, "and you are delightful in every way. I'm sorry, but my heart belongs to another."

I went and told Homer meeting another pug was not the answer. He winked at Nelly as we departed.

Homer and I walked back to his place. He said, "We need to get our minds off girls for a while. Let's just chill and watch TV."

"Homer, I'm not sure I want to watch *Best in Show* for the zillionth time," I said.

But the movie gave me an idea.

I went to a dog show, a warm-up contest for the Big Show. I thought maybe I could slide into the show ring, pass for a mastiff, and no one would notice. Wilson the Mastiff. I kind of liked the rhythm of it. Then Hedy and I would be a proper match.

lined up to be measured with the other mastiffs. I was off only by a little. I didn't think anyone really noticed. So far, so good.

I paraded around the ring with the other mastiffs, standing in line with them, looking straight ahead so as not to stand out.

It didn't work. The judge yelled, "You, in the yin-yang jacket! Out!"

I went back to Homer's place, where he was entertaining his rabbit friends.

He said, "I can't stop thinking about Nelly. The rabbits are teaching me a few things about flirting and courting. They're experts, you know."

I told the rabbits about my dilemma with Hedy and misadventure at the show. One of them said, "Our secret is that we're exactly alike," and then they hopped off to a dark, quiet corner to be alone.

Homer agreed to help me become more exactly like Hedy.

"**M**aybe this will straighten out your tail so it's more like Hedy's," said Homer, applying a warm iron. (Don't try this at home!) As excited as I was about the possibilities, my tail soon curled right back up again.

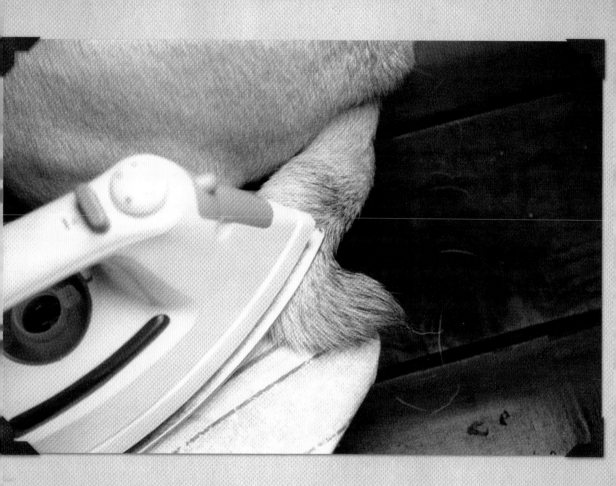

"**Y**ou'll need a bigger muzzle to look like Hedy," said Homer, sounding as though he had a terrible cold.

I was not so inspired.

"**Y**ou'll need to lose some of those wrinkles to look more like a mastiff," said Homer, sampling a little facial cream. Even though it cost a fortune, it didn't do a thing for his wrinkles.

Finally, Homer said, "You know, Wilson, I think you'll need to ask some actual big dogs about how to be a big dog."

He was right, and I went looking for my friends.

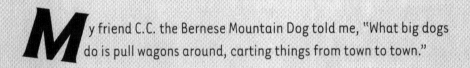

My friend C.C. the Bernese Mountain Dog told me, "What big dogs do is pull wagons around, carting things from town to town."

I tried pulling a wagon, but it wouldn't budge. I asked C.C., "Would you mind giving me a ride back into town instead?"

He obliged, and I thanked him.

Back in town, I visited my friend Arnold the German Shepherd, a police dog. He said, "A big dog rides around in a police car all day helping to keep the peace."

I hopped into Arnold's police car, but wasn't sure I was cut out for a life of fighting crime. I couldn't even see out the windows.

Arnold told me I'd also need a bigger, louder bark.

Arnold set me up with a bullhorn, which I barked into. But this didn't make me a big dog any more than it made me the first one in Berkeley to perch on top of a police car shouting into a megaphone.

I thanked Arnold and went to see my friend Big Eli.

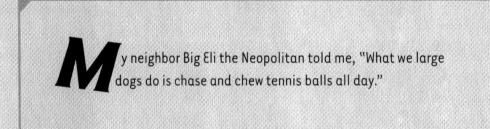

My neighbor Big Eli the Neopolitan told me, "What we large dogs do is chase and chew tennis balls all day."

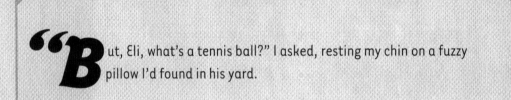

"**B**ut, Eli, what's a tennis ball?" I asked, resting my chin on a fuzzy pillow I'd found in his yard.

I stopped by the house of my good friend Henry the Coonhound, who said, "If you want to be a big dog, you need to learn how to drool, to really work up a good lather."

I looked into his mouth to see how this drooling was done, but I was as likely to be able to drool as I would be to whistle.

Idecided to consult my old acquaintance Roxy, a Hollywood pug who seemed to me a little larger than life. I got this message back from her assistant, a terrier named Lulu:

"Oh, romance is so complicated, darling. Whatever you do, get a prenup."

At this point, I decided I just needed to get in touch with my inner big dog.

resolved to do things that big dogs do. I tried chasing a stick on the beach but, frankly, I just didn't see the point.

Perhaps I needed a more cerebral approach.

I went to look at the books offering advice on relationships. But among the thousands of titles, there was not one piece of wisdom for a pug in love.

Then I remembered there is one self-help book for pugs.

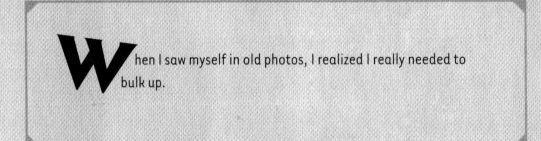

When I saw myself in old photos, I realized I really needed to bulk up.

I went the high-protein supplement route.

nd I spent hours at the gym. I might have gained a little muscle, but could do nothing about my stubborn center roll.

Still, I missed Hedy fiercely and thought about her constantly.

I couldn't concentrate. I went looking all over for my glasses when, in fact, they were on top of my head. Then I couldn't remember why I had glasses.

I couldn't eat. No matter how hard I tried to entice myself, all I could do was stare at the food on the plate.

I couldn't sleep. I tried counting sheep, but I kept getting stuck at "One . . . two . . . oh, Hedy, my sweet little lamb."

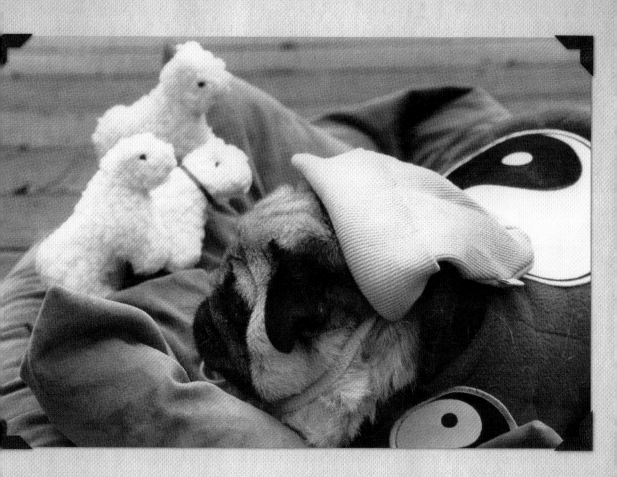

All I could do was sit around and compose songs about my love for Hedy.

But I knew the day of the Big Show was fast approaching.

On the day of the Big Show, I knew I would lose Hedy forever. She was a shoo-in to win the championship and be wedded to Shakespeare, as had been arranged.

I was lovesick and could do nothing but lie in bed, staring at Hedy's picture, remembering that day we shared in the park.

I had to at least see her one last time.

I went to the Big Show. Not knowing what to do, I sat there doing nothing because, as it is written, "*For those who practice not-doing, everything will fall into place.*"

While I was sitting there doing nothing, Greta approached me. We looked on as the mastiffs, including Hedy, began to line up to enter the ring.

Greta said, "Oh, Wilson, how I wish I could win the Big Show and become betrothed to Shakespeare the Stud, with whom I am madly in love. But I am not beautiful like Hedy, as I am without 'marked wrinkles, which are particularly distinctive.' "

Instead, Hedy will win the show today and be forever united with Shakespeare. But she is so in love with you. It will surely break her heart." She looked to the ring, adding, "Oh, never mind. The show is about to begin," as she began to walk away.

I had an idea.

"**G**reta, wait!" I called after her. "Come closer. I can show you how to make marked wrinkles, which are particularly distinctive. Then you can switch places with Hedy in the show. You will surely win the championship and be united with Shakespeare. And Hedy and I can *enjoy the plain and simple*."

"Yes, yes," she said, "show me, show me!"

"Think of something really puzzling. Like this"—I showed her, as my wrinkles became more marked and particularly distinctive. "For instance, try to understand why humans do the things they do."

Greta thought and puzzled on this, and as she did so, I watched her wrinkles grow more marked and particularly distinctive.

"That's it!" I said. "Now go to Hedy and trade places with her. Hurry, Greta, the mastiffs are entering the ring!"

Greta caught Hedy just before she entered the ring and quickly told her the plan. They secretly traded places.

Shakespeare looked on in awe of Greta, his would-be bride, parading magnificently around the ring with her marked wrinkles, which were particularly distinctive. Hedy also looked on, thrilled for her sister. They both hoped she would win, though for very different reasons, of course.

When the judge said, "Number one!" and pointed to Greta, a great howl went up, the loudest from Shakespeare and Hedy.

I cheered, too, but more quietly. Inside, I was singing the most beautiful song.

I met Hedy back at her house after the show, presenting her with a plateful of special cookies. We shared them, just as she had once dreamed we might.

Meanwhile, Homer was off enjoying himself at a pug party, where he was seen canoodling with Nelly the Pug. The rabbits had given him a few good pointers.

Hedy said, "Oh, Wilson, I am so glad we can finally be together. But how did you know not to give up?"

"The Master acts on what he feels and not what he sees," I said, then asked her, "whatever did you see in me, a diminutive little pug?"

She said, "You're just you, Wilson the Pug, and I'm more than okay with that."

And we had ourselves a little snuggle.

I gave Hedy a new, better fitting yin-yang jacket. She brought me into her home where we would *enjoy the plain and simple* for the rest of our lives.

Afterword

Fortunately, I was a neutered pug, because Hedy and I felt strongly that the world didn't need a new breed of mastug or pugstiff.

Acknowledgments

*"Those who do things well will be honored from
generation to generation."*

—TAO-TE CHING, 54

So many people did so many things so well in bringing this book to
life. We wish to honor all of them here: our creative and business
teammates at Viking Studio, especially our most trusted editor,

Alessandra Lusardi, for her unique understanding of Wilson's wisdom and voice; Megan Newman, who appreciated the idea of canine love right off the bat; Kate Stark, whose creative approach to business is inspiring; Jessica Lee, who steadies the ship; Molly Brouillette for her relentless but diplomatic pursuit; the always-visionary Clare Ferarro for her keen foresight; and all the talented copy editors, artists and designers who assemble the pieces, especially Daniel Lagin for his lovely design. Special thanks to our good friend and Wilson's favorite agent, Arielle Eckstut, and everyone at the Levine Greenberg Literary Agency.

For their unwavering patience and creative contribution, we are forever grateful to Sarah Child, Aimee Child, and the magnificent mastiffs of Heritage Hearth Mastiffs of Walnut Creek, California, www.hhmastiffs.com, especially Hedy, Greta, Shakespeare, and Mighty Mo.

For their very generous cooperation, we wish to extend our deepest
gratitude to the always photogenic Roxy and her kind staff, Mary
Steenburgen, Ted Danson, Charlie McDowell, Kevin Keating, and Alison
Mann for her art direction; and Lisa Sheeran, Frisco Pugs, and the
beautiful Nina, AKA Ch. Frisco's D'Lightful Dancer.

For their kind support, we thank Jenna Elfman and Gwen and Willy;
Tori Spelling and Mimi La Rue; Lili Taylor and Gulliver; Marv and
Heather Albert and Lulu and Ruby; MuchLove Animal Rescue; and Sony
Pictures Entertainment. Special thanks to Rosie the Riveting Pit Bull,
who reminds us to spay and neuter.

Many thanks to Michael Levy and Pet Food Express, the Courthouse
Athletic Club, Berkeley Police Department, Emeryville Police
Department, Optimum Nutrition, Rachel Goodenow and Obadiah
Tarzan Greenberg, in loving memory of the regal Eli the Neopolitan

Mastiff, Wilson's oldest friend, Henry the Coonhound with Tamara Romijn and Oh Henry, www.carcoverall.com, Ch.Best Bets Cash Advance, CGC, the stately Bernese Mountain Dog owned and loved by Mike and Terri Whalen, Larry Bohlig and Chief the brilliant Bernese Mountain Dog, the Albatross (Wilson's favorite Berkeley pub), Pottery Barn Kids for their unique growth chart ruler, Aimee Chitayat and her piano, Terence Davis for his musical inspiration, Barnes & Noble of El Cerrito, California, the good people of PhotoLab and Cantoo Photo, and Pawsitively Gourmet, www.pawsitivelygourmet.com, for their delicious yin-yang cookies.

We were once again fortunate to have the opportunity to work with a real master of her craft: Iris Davis of Davis Black and White. No one makes Wilson and friends look better. For their loving support, we thank our circle of friends, with special appreciation to Homer's best friend, Catherine Woodman. Thank you to Nancy's dear cousin Gary Hoffman, for encouraging the original idea. To Nancy's mother, Eileen Levine, late father, Irwin H. Levine, and sister, Fran Herault, thank you for providing fertile ground in which love could take root.